CHANGE THE WAY YOU SEE EVERYTHING

THROUGH ASSET-BASED THINKING

FOR TEENS

Asset-based® Thinking

Asset-Based Thinking is the copyrighted property of:

The Concept Farm

Published by Running Press Kids, an imprint of
Running Press Book Publishers
2300 Chestnut Street
Philadelphia, PA 19103-4371

Visit us on the web:
www.runningpress.com
www.assetbasedthinking.com

9 8 7 6 5 4 3 2 1
Digit on the right indicates the number of this printing
Library of Congress Control Number: 2008933261
ISBN 978-07624-3350-6

CHANGE THE WAY YOU SEE EVERYTHING

THROUGH ASSET-BASED THINKING

FOR TEENS

KATHRYN D. CRAMER, Ph.D. & HANK WASIAK

Founder & Managing Partner, *The Cramer Institute*   Co-Founder, *The Concept Farm*

RP | TEENS
PHILADELPHIA · LONDON

CONTENTS

James Patterson

THE CRAMER INSTITUTE
231 S. BEMISTON SUITE 102
ST. LOUIS, MISSOURI 63105

6

I am a writer and have published over 50 books. By way of explaining why I do what I do, let me tell you a story from my youth.

When I was your age, growing up in Newburgh, NY, my grandfather had a business delivering ice cream and frozen food. He used to drive his truck over the Storm King Mountain and occasionally he would bring me along.

Whenever he would go over the mountain, he'd sing and one day I asked him why. He turned to me and gave me the best advice of my life. He told me that he didn't care whether I became president of the United States, a ditch digger, or a truck driver. Only one thing was important. "When you go up over the mountain to your work every morning, make sure you are singing. The same way I am in this broken-down ice cream truck. I am happy, Jim. I love my work."

So, I'm passing that advice along to you. Sing. Be happy. And, I'm adding a little advice of my own. The same advice I've given my son, Jack. Read. Become a passionate reader for life, and not because you have to or because it might make you more successful. I'm talking about real passion here, like the way you currently go crazy over THE SIMPSONS, THE INCREDIBLES, and PlayStation. It's true that books can make you crazy, but in a good way. Read because you love to, not because you have to, and books will bring you happiness every day of your life, for the rest of your life.

That's one of the reasons I wrote a whole series of books just for teens that you might have heard about . . . Maximum Ride. The books are filled with great examples of Asset-Based Thinking in action, which I think you might like hearing about from Max, the main character. You will meet Max in Chapter 2.

Enjoy!

James Patterson

How We Got Here. We Thought You Should Know.

The book you're reading now is very special because just about everything about it involved YOU!

The idea was inspired by teens. In workshops around the country, teens like you opened our eyes to new and exciting ways to apply Asset-Based Thinking. Teens like you kept us grounded in the reality of your world. Most of the photographs in the book were taken by teens. Check out your creativity and imagination in the stories and quotes from other teens.

Change the Way You See Everything – a book by and for teens.

Enjoy and be proud of joining our ABT teen team!

Kathy & Hank

P.S. We also created two other best-selling adult books about Asset-Based Thinking (*Change the Way You See Everything* and *Change the Way You See Yourself*). ABT is already making a positive difference in the world. As you and your friends become Asset-Based Thinkers, the power of ABT will grow exponentially. Thank you for making a positive difference in your world!

Bryanne Leeming

To: Kathy & Hank
From: Bryanne

5-3-06

"On one particular jog from the kitchen to my room, I noticed a book I'd never seen before sitting on the table and something about it caught my eye. The title, 'Change the Way You See Everything,' was backwards and the book had lots of cool pictures and titles. Even though it was aimed at adults and not kids my age, I was hooked before I even read the phrase 'Asset-Based Thinking.'

Although the adult situations in the book may not always apply to the life of a teenager, it was easy for me to connect them to situations in my own life. Getting a promotion could be getting moved up from JV to Varsity in a sport and the experience of parenting a teenager could be like taking care of a pet. So even though the book is written for adults, teens can read it and change things around in their mind to represent their lives. I think it is very beneficial for kids and teens to read about Asset-Based Thinking. It will help us throughout our lives and starting now will only make it easier. I started the book without ever having heard of ABT and by the end I was already trying to practice it in my life."

Here's Bryanne's letter (written at age 15) about our first book that inspired this book.

CHAPTER 1

ABT

GETTING STARTED

READY. SET. GO...

SOMETIMES
AWFUL...

SOMETIMES
AWESOME!

ALWAYS
A D b T

WHAT IS ABT?

ASSET + **BASED** + **THINKING**

Something or somebody that is useful and contributes to the success of something.

Principle or starting point of a system or theory.

Use of the mind to form thoughts, opinions, or conclusions.

WHAT IS DBT?

DEFICIT + BASED + THINKING

DEFICIT
A term that refers to something negative, something you want less of, something you don't value.

BASED
Principle or starting point of a system or theory.

THINKING
Use of the mind to form thoughts, opinions, or conclusions.

Of course, there's another way to SEE . . .
and that's through the lens of negative thoughts.
While positive thoughts make you feel good and
help you be more creative and happy, negative
thoughts make you feel uneasy, worried, upset —
they hold you back. This type of negative "seeing"
is called deficit-based thinking (DBT).

EMPHASIZE THE POSITIVE

WHAT IF... You could see what is strong and right about yourself more often than what might be weak or wrong? Just think how cool that would be!

WHAT IF... You could focus on what you like and admire about your friends, family, teachers, and coaches, rather than what sometimes frustrates or disappoints you? Just think how amazing that would be!

WHAT IF... You could view any situation – whether boring or challenging, expected or unexpected, awesome or awful – as a chance to learn and make yourself more confident and capable? Just think how awesome that would be!

How you see things can actually make just about everything in your life better. SEEING what's best about everyone and everything (including YOU) is what we call Asset-Based Thinking, or ABT. *With ABT you can turn "what if" into "what is."*

All it takes is some practice, a little attitude shift, and your imagination.

TAKE A LOOK...

FROM DBT

TOO HARD . . . .

REALLY WEIRD . . . .

I HATE THAT . . . .

I AM CLUELESS . . . .

I DON'T WANT TO . . . .

NO WAY . . . .

I WISH I COULD . . . .

THIS IS SO STRANGE . . . .

TO ABT

SO CHALLENGING . . . .

SO RARE . . . .

I LOVE THIS . . . .

I DON'T KNOW YET . . . .

I DO WANT TO . . . .

THIS WAY . . . .

I'M GLAD I CAN . . . .

THIS IS SO UNUSUAL . . . .

QUIT BEING SO . . . .

STOP THAT . . . .

YOU SHOULDN'T . . . .

I'M JEALOUS OF YOU BECAUSE . . . .

I DON'T LIKE THAT . . . .

WHAT'S SO AWFUL IS . . . .

START BEING MORE . . . .

TRY THIS . . . .

YOU COULD . . . .

I ADMIRE YOU BECAUSE . . . .

I LIKE THIS BETTER . . . .

WHAT'S SO AMAZING IS . . . .

WHICH
MOOD O YOU CHOOSE?

Try imagining how different situations will call for shifting from DBT to ABT. It's a shift that is sure to give your mood a lift. Five examples are listed on the chart. Think of five more. Notice how ABT comments create mood uplifts and how DBT comments trigger mood downers.

SITUATIONS	MOOD DOWNERS DBT Comments	UPSIDE MOOD UPLIFTS ABT Comments
When the exam is tougher than you expected	"This exam is too hard."	"This exam is so challenging."
When you meet someone with an unusual personality	"She is so weird."	"She is so unique."
When someone bothers you	"Stop that."	"Try this."
When you see someone excel	"I am jealous of you because . . ."	"I admire you because . . ."
When you are not sure of yourself	"I'm scared."	"I've never felt this way."

DBT DOWNSIDE

WHAT YOU GET IS WHAT YOU SEE. WHAT YOU SEE...

If you SEE and trust in the positive ABT side of life, you grow more sure of yourself; you feel happier and more energetic. You're like the Energizer Bunny that just keeps on going and going and you get more out of every day. Other people want to be with you. You get along better with everyone.

You're part of the action.

SEEING the best in whatever happens increases your influence over how things turn out. SEEING what's good — even about bad situations — helps you bounce back more quickly from setbacks and mistakes. And when you really look for what is possible, new opportunities come your way.

STARTS A **BIG** CHAIN REACTION

What you SEE determines what you THINK. What you think drives what you SAY, which in turn influences what you DO. This whole big chain reaction starts with what YOU SEE.

SEEING+THINKING+SPEAKING+ACTING=

A = BEING ABT

HERE'S HOW THE ABT CHAIN REACTION WORKS:

I see	I think	I say	I do	I am
MY CORRECT TEST ANSWERS	I'VE LEARNED A LOT	I LIKE THIS CLASS	MORE READING	PROUD OF MYSELF
SOMEONE RECYCLE	THAT'S GOOD FOR THE ENVIRONMENT	THANK YOU	REMEMBER TO RECYCLE	MORE RESPONSIBLE

"You have brains in your head.
You have feet in your shoes.
You can steer yourself in any
direction you choose."
~Dr. Seuss

THINK ABOUT YOUR THINKING...

Thinking comes naturally. It's automatic. You don't have to put much effort into thinking – it seems as if thoughts just happen. But the truth is that you can control your thoughts, if you know how to think about your thinking. Thoughts are made up of words, images, and feelings about whatever is happening to you. They reveal how you SEE everything in your world. Your thoughts are powerful. They impact everything – how much you learn, how much others like you, how you influence others, how you handle situations, and how happy you are.

You can actually teach yourself how to think about your thinking.

Sounds complicated but it isn't. It's fun to do. By learning to be an Asset-Based Thinker you can change your thoughts into superpowers that work for you.

29

NETWORKS IN YOUR MIND

Pretend for just a moment that your mind is a television station broadcasting programs on only two networks — the ABT network and the DBT network. The ABT network features positive program thoughts. The DBT network features negative program thoughts.

Now imagine that you have a remote control that allows you to tune into either network anytime. You're in control. Anytime you want to, no matter what is happening to you, with this remote control you could tune into the ABT thought channel or the DBT thought channel . . . It's all up to you.

Here's the best part: You run the networks, own the TV set, and operate the remote that controls it all. Think of the remote as a very real symbol of your power to decide which channel you will tune into — either the ABT or DBT network. It works every time you use it. How you SEE, what you LOOK at and LISTEN to, is your choice.

THINK TWICE

For each topic, review your best and worst thoughts. Every topic broadcasts both positive and negative thoughts in your mind. The best and worst sides are both true at the same time. It's your choice, and yours alone, to decide on which side you want to focus — the best or the worst. What you pay attention to gives you the power to change the channel from one network to the other. You have the power to spend more time on the ABT network or the DBT network. It's up to you!

BE HONEST **THINK** AND FEEL YOUR RESPONSES. ——

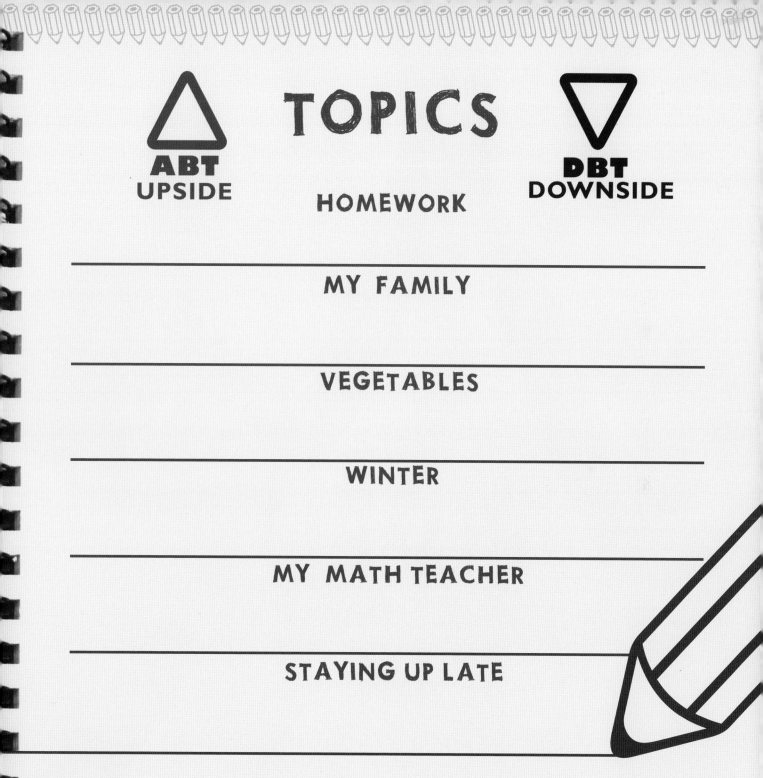

TOPICS

ABT UPSIDE

DBT DOWNSIDE

HOMEWORK

MY FAMILY

VEGETABLES

WINTER

MY MATH TEACHER

STAYING UP LATE

5

GIMME
FIVE!

The best way to make sure you are tuned into the ABT network is to spend your time and effort looking for assets (e.g., what's good, what's interesting, what's right, what's strong, what's best) about:

YOURSELF
OTHER PEOPLE
AND WHATEVER HAPPENS

Even if things aren't perfect, the more you see and pay attention to what is good and positive about everything in your life, the happier and more capable you will be.

THE 5 TO 1 RULE:

Train yourself to spend more time thinking about assets than you do about deficits. In whatever situation you encounter, focus on the positives first and try to list as many of them as you can. If you can get to 5, great. Then, when you think about the negatives, try to narrow them down to the 1 that is the biggest. Let those 5 to 1 thoughts lead you through your day, every day. By doing your best to tune in to the ABT network 5 times more than you do to the DBT network, you slowly but surely become an Asset-Based Thinker.

Research shows that people who tune into ABT most of the day are more attractive, satisfied, and get more done than people who tune in to DBT more often. Asset-Based Thinkers are just cooler, period!

TELL YOURSELF AN **ABT** BEDTIME STORY

Before you fall asleep, remind yourself of what made your day a good day — maybe even a great day.

Maybe someone else made your day by being funny or generous.

Maybe you achieved a goal or did something that helped you feel confident or smart.

Maybe a class, conversation, or game turned out to be better than you thought it would.

Maybe you discovered a new type of food that you really like.

Maybe you helped someone else have a good day.

No matter how big or small your daily assets may be, when you fall asleep counting them you will sleep better and wake up in an ABT mood, ready to make tomorrow a great day, too.

COUNT OFF 5 REASONS WHY YOUR DAY WAS GREAT.

REASON 1 _____

REASON 2 _____

REASON 3 _____

REASON 4 _____

REASON 5 _____

Note: If you've had a really bad day, add one more chapter. Think of the one thing you could change for the better tomorrow. This ABT "tomorrow improvement" will help make your dreams come true.

CHAPTER 2
CHANGE THE WAY YOU SEE YOU
THE DEEPER YOU LOOK... THE MORE YOU FIND.

Now it's time to get a good ABT look at yourself. One of the best ways to do that is to view yourself from the outside in, the inside out, and from different angles. By doing this, you are able to get a whole new perspective on all the things that make you . . . YOU. In ABT terms, it's your "Personal Package." It's made up of various assets that you take with you out into the world, every day.

THE ASSETS THAT GO INTO YOUR PERSONAL PACKAGE ARE:

1. <u>Your Mind</u>: intelligence and imagination

2. <u>Your Heart</u>: caring and concern for other people

3. <u>Your Body</u>: physical well-being and appearance

4. <u>Your Spirit</u>: values and beliefs

5. <u>Your Skills</u>: behavior and abilities

Everyone has a unique combination of these personal assets. As an Asset-Based Thinker, you owe it to yourself to take an in-depth look into each one of your personal assets. Looking at your assets is fun and builds confidence. The more clearly you see what makes you You, the more you can accomplish and contribute, and the more full and fulfilled your personal package becomes.

GIVE YOURSELF  5 A's

DISCOVER YOUR STAR POWER

Imagine this feeling: You've been training with your friends for the next BMX race. This time it all paid off and you won. Everybody is cheering, including you. Or, you study hard for days to make sure you pass a big exam in one of your most challenging subjects. It's grade time. Your teacher calls you to the front of the class and announces, "Not only did you pass, you got an A." YES! Getting an "A" is fantastic anytime. It's especially great when you've studied so hard and overcome one of your toughest challenges, and get to take a bow and as a bonus, be recognized.

With ABT, you can get that same kind of feeling by studying your Personal Assets just as diligently as you would study for that challenging test. Think of your five types of assets (Mind, Heart, Body, Spirit, and Skills) as important subjects you need to learn in order to be proud of and excited to be the person you are. After you study each Personal Asset, you can give yourself an "A" for the strengths and positive qualities you find and value in yourself.

FIRST: Think about each Personal Asset on the list below. Read the qualities and strengths that are associated with the 5 types of Personal Assets.

SECOND: Circle 3 of the qualities or strengths that best describe you for each asset category.

THIRD: Discover the star you are by writing the three strengths or qualities you possess under each of your Personal Assets. Place your photo in the center of the star. You may want to copy your star onto another piece of paper or poster board and hang it up someplace where you can see it every day. Be sure to take a good look at your ABT stars and see the amazing person you are.

Your Mind:	**Your Heart:**	**Your Body:**	**Your Spirit:**	**Your Skills:**
alert	caring	energetic	honest	athletic
decisive	compassionate	attractive	faithful	artistic
learns well	helpful	strong	fair	gardening
solves problems	agreeable	healthy	trustworthy	cooking
reads well	friendly	flexible	abundant	musical
open-minded	loyal	well-rested	grateful	singing
creative	devoted	well-nourished	resilient	speaking
imaginative	peacemaker	beautiful	vibrant	technical
sense of humor	patient	lean	enduring	dancing
analytical	tolerant	fit	authentic	writing

SEE THE STAR YOU ARE.

1. Your Mind:
_____
_____
_____
_____

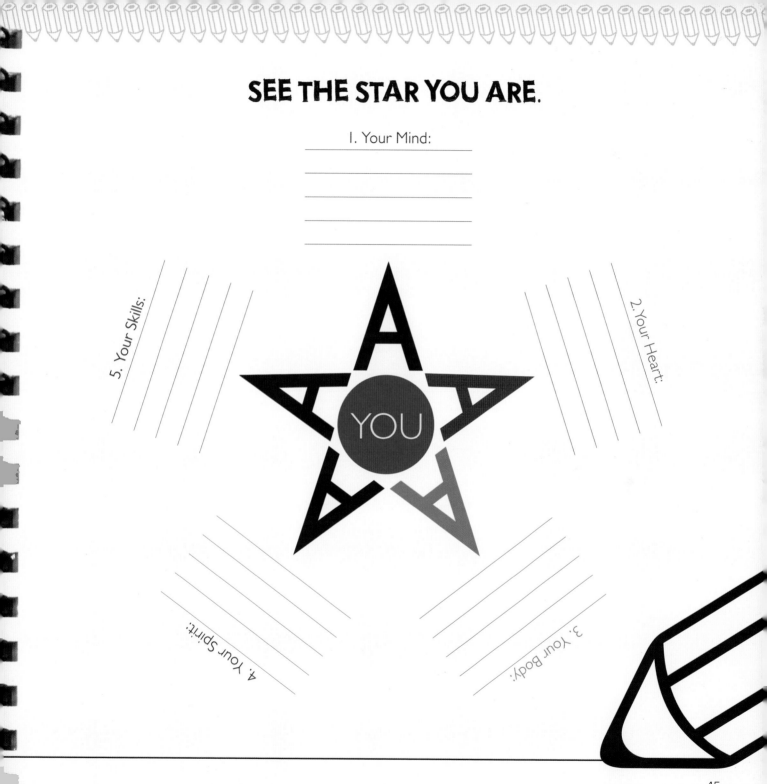

5. Your Skills:

2. Your Heart:

YOU

4. Your Spirit:

3. Your Body:

COACH DON'T CRITICIZE.

Often, it's easier to see what you don't like about yourself than what you do. When you pay too much attention to your mistakes, flaws, or shortcomings, you wind up criticizing yourself. As you probably have guessed already, criticizing yourself means you are on the DBT (Deficit-Based Thinking) network. Think of self-criticism as a DBT program full of negative stories about you.

Self-criticism demoralizes and disappoints you. It's a downer. Criticizing yourself too much or too often puts you in a bad mood and robs you of the confidence you need to get through your day. When you find yourself on the DBT network, viewing a negative side of yourself, it's time to take out your ABT remote and change the channel.

One quick way to shift from a DBT view of yourself to the ABT side is to notice how your best qualities, strengths, and talents help you succeed and solve problems. When you see how valuable your Personal Assets can be, you will wind up coaching yourself to use them. Coaching yourself means you're tuned into the positive programming on the ABT (Asset-Based Thinking) network. ABT programs zero in on what a talented and capable person you are. The stories you see about yourself will encourage and amaze you. The ABT network features the best of who you are and how you put your assets to work.

GET IN TOUCH WITH YOUR PERSONAL COACH

Here's a quick exercise to be sure you are tuning in to the ABT channel for viewing the best sides of yourself.

YOUR MIND:

I know I am intelligent because

_____

My powers of imagination are amazing when I

_____

YOUR HEART:

I am a good friend when I

_____

When someone is hurt or angry, I show concern by

_____

YOUR BODY:

When I am healthy, my body feels

_____

YOUR SPIRIT:

I know I am being my best self when I

_____

Telling the truth works for me because

_____

YOUR SKILL:

I am particularly skillful when it comes to

_____

I am proud of being able to

_____

Now, turn up the volume on your ABT channel and read each sentence you completed out loud to yourself. Listen carefully to what you are saying. Next, repeat each sentence silently in your mind. Pay close attention to how you feel as you repeat the sentences silently to yourself.

What you say to yourself silently is just as powerful as what you say out loud — sometimes even more so. Think of the positive messages you say to yourself as a way of coaching yourself from the inside with your mind.

Building the positive power of your internal coach is very important. When things are going well, your internal coach can celebrate your accomplishments and increase your self-confidence by pointing out what you did to be successful. Make your positive internal coach one of your constant companions and most trusted assets . . . right up there with family, best friends, teachers, and mentors. Your "go to" person who is on call just for you.

CALL THIS YOUR "INTERNAL COACH," YOUR "GO TO" PERSON.

CELEBRATE SUCCESS FROM THE **IN**SIDE OUT.

Give your internal coach a chance to celebrate you and your success by thinking about a time when things turned out for the best. Maybe you achieved a goal, made a good decision that really paid off, spoke up for something you believed in, came to the aid of a friend, or something else. Ask your internal coach to describe how you used your assets to succeed.

How did I use my intelligence and imagination?

_____

How did I show care and concern for others?

_____

How did my body help me?

_____

How was I true to my values?

_____

Another great thing – your internal coach is not just a "fair-weather friend" who is there for you only when things are going well. Even when things are not going so well, your internal coach can give you encouragement and help you solve your problems. For example, problems occur when you make a mistake, develop a bad habit, hurt someone's feelings, or forget to do your homework. Coaching yourself helps you solve problems. Criticizing yourself just makes your problems worse and makes you feel worse about them!

You can't avoid problems. Problems are a part of everyone's lives. Some are big; some are small. Some problems last a long time and some you can solve quickly. No matter what their size, shape, or duration, ABT can help you coach yourself to a solution.

Maddy Acaro (signature)

Let's take a look at how 14-year-old Maddy used ABT to coach herself into being healthier, gaining control over her weight, and fulfilling her desire to be her best at a sport she loves.

HOW I EARNED MY STARS

I earned my stars by taking control of a serious weight issue I had so that I could enjoy life more and be the best athlete I could be. Since the age of nine I have struggled with my weight. Every summer I would promise myself that this would be the summer that I would lose the weight, but I never did. However, last summer was different. I made the decision to put the 5 years of torture to an end. I decided to set the goal of losing all the extra weight I had gained over past years. The entire summer I worked my heart out by working out every day and eating healthily. French fries and grilled cheeses suddenly became chicken, fruit, and veggies. And doughnuts and other sweets were replaced with healthy protein shakes and Jell-O. Although there was much sweat and many tears, it was all worth it, for now I have lost approximately 70 pounds. I now believe in a healthy and active lifestyle, and sports are a major part of that. Playing soccer is my favorite form of exercise because it's not only calorie-burning, but it's a fun way to lose weight. I now can encourage others with my story so they can be motivated to lose weight, too. I believe in all of those people who are struggling with the same issues I had and believe that with determination they can also reach their goal.

TRY THIS

COACH YOURSELF TO EARN YOUR
STARS

Now it's your turn. Think of ways you behave that create problems for you. Which behaviors do you want to change? Watching too much TV? Eating too many snacks? Arguing with your parents? Messing up your room? Neglecting your homework?

STEP 1:

Face the truth about your behavior (how big, how long, how important).
State your goal in one sentence.

_____

STEP 2:

See the talents, skills, and strengths you possess to change your behavior and to reach your
goal. List 3 to 5 Personal Assets you will tap.

_____

_____

_____

STEP 3:

Take action to alter your behavior and to achieve positive results – for yourself and for
other people. Name the actions you will take.

_____

ASPIRATION BEFORE PERSPIRATION

Camille Shuken

"I love my horse. My passion is riding. I want us to take first place together."

When it comes to coaching yourself to solve problems, ABT is always there for you. You, like Camille, can find that ABT is indispensable (which means you can't live without it) for tuning into the things you love the most (Your Passions) and discovering your deepest dreams and desires (Your Aspirations). Aspirations are essential to your happiness and are aimed at realizing possibilities, not solving problems. And when aspirations are linked to your passions, the possibilities are endless. Aspirations: **Don't leave home without them!**

ASPIRATION IS WHAT YOU DESIRE FOR YOURSELF.

ASPIRATION GIVES LIFE A LIFT.

ASPIRATION FILLS YOU WITH ANTICIPATION AND POSSIBILITIES.

PUT YOURSELF ON THE
RED CARPET

Pretend for just a moment that you are on the red carpet of a big premiere event starring You. The cameras are flashing, fans are happy to be there, and you are being interviewed by your favorite television host. You are thrilled to be there and everyone is so excited to see you and get to know who you are. The host begins the interview by asking, "What matters most to you and what makes you tick? What are your deepest desires and greatest aspirations for yourself?" What would you say? Jot down some of your first unfiltered thoughts to these red carpet questions now.

The things that I really love and care about the most are:

_____

My aspirations for myself are:

_____

The host says, "Tell me why these aspirations are important to you?" You say, "These aspirations are important to me because:"

_____

Then the host asks, "How will your life be better? How will you be better off if you achieve your aspirations?" You reflect a moment and then say, "My life will be better and I will be better because:"

_____

And one more time the host probes deeper. "Tell me what would be possible if you achieved your aspirations that is not possible now? What would be different and so much better?" You take a deep breath before you answer and then you say, "What would be possible and better is:"

_____

ER STAGE!

The imaginary interview at your premiere event is a perfect way for you to discover yourself and your aspirations. Step into the spotlight and interview yourself whenever you need inspiration and to give your life a lift.

You could even tailor the interview to focus on specific types of Personal Assets. For example, you could zero in on your aspirations for enhancing your mind or your heart or your body, or your spirit or your skills. **Be creative . . . have fun! Give yourself a lift. Aim for the stars. Aspire.**

MEET MAX ★

Age 14 and Leader of the Flock

For those of you who may not be familiar with me or my flock, here are the essentials: We're part of a complex experiment that has altered our DNA, our very genetic structure. We're 98% human but 2% avian. That 2% has had a dramatic effect on us. Some effects are visible, like my 12-foot wingspan; others are not. We're all stronger, lighter, and faster than any 100% human out there. Cool, right? It especially comes in handy when you spend your days running from scientists who want to capture you and exploit your special abilities. (OK . . . Assets.)

But what does this have to do with you, or Asset-Based Thinking, for that matter? This book and ABT would have come in handy years ago when we first escaped from the lab that created us. As it turns out, in dealing with our adversities and challenges, we've all learned some important ABT lessons. So, as you flip through these pages, like me, you'll learn how to deal with pretty much anything life throws at you. I've listed a few ABT tips that have helped me:

MAX ABT TIPS

- *Always keep your cool.* Regardless of what's going on around you, taking a minute to think things through can save you hours of problems and make dealing with things easier. Easy is always better.

- *Have a goal, plan, and think ahead.* Sure, stuff may unfold differently, but once you're certain of what you want to get done, it's a heck of a lot easier to make it happen, trust me.

- *Be proud and act proud every day.* Your individual assets make you unique. Not necessarily better or worse than anyone else . . . just uniquely YOU (and, boy, do I know what it is to be unique!). Be proud of your uniqueness and do things everyday that make you proud of yourself.

- *Fly with people you trust.* Surround yourself with people you can count on and make sure that they know they can count on you.

PASSIONS
+ ACTIONS
+ ASPIRATIONS
= LIVING YOUR
DREAM

ASPIRATIONS INSPIRE

If you love learning and aspire to be a better student, you take action to study more often and more diligently. If you love sports and aspire to be a better soccer player, you practice longer and take more shots on goal. If you love music and aspire to learn to play the piano, you act on that aspiration by taking piano lessons. When you get in touch with your passions and act on your aspirations, you come alive AND start living your dreams. Life stops being boring or ordinary or a drag. You're up and aware. You have a starring role in whatever happens. You see yourself succeeding before your very eyes. The next best you comes into view . . . for you and everyone around you. Now that's what being an ABT STAR is all about!

Having time to yourself to do whatever you want is an important part of living and enjoying life. Everything from playing a video game to reading a book, from drawing a picture or skateboarding to just sitting and staring out the window – it's all important. Asset-Based Thinkers learn to enjoy "**ABT You Time.**" It takes you to a very special place that you create.

Imagine yourself traveling by car, train, plane, or bike on your way to your great adventure. See yourself crossing vast expanses of land and oceans or soaring through the air on your snowboard. It is just as important to keep track of where you've been as it is to watch where you're going. Every milestone of progress, every setback, every unexpected breakdown or bit of good luck teaches you valuable lessons for how to navigate the challenges that lie ahead.

TURN EXPERIENCES INTO WHAT ASSET-BASED THINKERS CALL "MEGA MOMENTS."

With ABT, you can learn to imagine the biggest and most important moments of your own life as a great adventure. You can learn to see your own life experience as one of your best teachers.

CREATE YOUR OWN MEGA MOMENT MAP

 ENVISION YOUR MEGA MOMENTS

Use ABT to reflect on Mega Moments in your life and what you learned from each memorable Mega Moment. This will help you get to know yourself better. You will be able to see what worked and what didn't. This will help you know how to spot and best respond to Mega Moments in the future.

 THEN SEE YOUR MEGA MOMENT MAP IN YOUR MIND

Think of this type of reflection as creating a mental map of the Mega Moments of your life. This Mega Moment Map will remind you of the important things that have happened to you and how they have shaped you into the unique and amazingly special person you are. As you create your Mega Moment Map, you are investing in You Time. Time devoted exclusively to seeing the incredible person you are becoming and how much you already know about the way life works.

NOW BRING YOUR MAP TO LIFE:

Creating a map of the Mega Moments of your life will be a new, exciting, and creative experience for you. Approach it with all the curiosity, energy, and spirit of discovery you can find in yourself. Here are the "how to" basics to get you started . . . then improvise all you want.

Assemble pens, pencils, colored markers, and paper long enough to make a timeline in one-year increments, from your birth to your current age (shelf paper about 2 feet long works well).

Next, draw a horizontal line across your page. Make tick-marks about 2 to 3 inches apart along the horizontal line to represent each year of your life, from your first year up until your age right now. Now spend 20 to 30 minutes reflecting on the Mega Moments of your life. Remember valuable experiences that have made an impression on you and taught you some kind of lesson. Remember as far back as you can (most people do remember a few Mega Moments from as far back as 3 or 4 years old).

THIS IS YOUR YOU TIME.
HAVE FUN AND GO FOR IT!

BABY GIRL

First big trip: Maine

Started pre-school
1 2 3
- - - - - - - - -
Went to a family Eunion in South Dakota

Luau-themed birthday party

my birthday!

my first time on an air-plane

Great Aunt Karen

Started kindergarten

Me!

AE

Here's an example of a Mega Moments Map created by Claire when she was almost 12 years old. Pretty cool. Use it for inspiration.

Claire Marie

Olympics-themed birthday party

Went to a new school and made lots & new friends

7 · 8 · 9 · 10 · 11

ead one the Scripture dings **at my** t Holy munion

Went to the Poconos with my relatives and family.

SACRED HEART SCHOOL

Got braces!!!

- - - - - - - -

Swam with stingrays in the Grand Cayman Islands

After you craft your Mega Moments Map, you're ready to enjoy the next part of your adventure. Sit back and think about what each experience meant to you. What did you learn? Then, write the lesson on your map or in a journal. Reflect on each Mega Moment one at a time. You should do this on your own schedule . . . in one sitting, over several days or even several weeks. Make the most of it.

Finally, it's a great idea to share your Mega Moments Map with a friend or family member. When you hear yourself telling the story of each of those moments, you learn even more about yourself and about life. Also, the person you share them with will thoroughly enjoy the experience with you.

TRUST YOURSELF AND OTHERS WILL, TOO.

TO TRUST SOMEONE MEANS YOU

BELIEVE IN ...
RELY ON ...
DEPEND ON ...

THAT PERSON. You know you trust someone when you are willing to put your faith in what the person says and does. You count on people you trust to keep promises and live up to commitments. It's natural not to trust everyone. You trust people who you feel are trustworthy and have earned your trust.

WHO DO YOU TRUST?

Think about members of your family, close friends, teachers, teammates — the people you really trust. Write down their names and make a note of what they have done to earn your trust.

Some examples of what people do to earn your trust may include keeping secrets, keeping promises, following through, telling the truth, showing loyalty, avoiding gossip, backing you up or standing up for other people's beliefs.

PEOPLE I TRUST:

HOW THEY HAVE EARNED MY TRUST:

_____

_____

_____

_____

Let your creative juices flow and write something amazing ... an ABT Acrostic.

ACROSTIC

A

B ....

T ....

Acrostic is probably a new word for you. (Use it to impress your friends and family!) It's simple, fun, and interesting to do. Think of it as a 5-line poem or rap verse about what trust means to you. Use the letters that spell *trust* as the first letter of each word that begins a line.

MAKE YOURS HERE:

T ....

R ....

U ....

S ....

T ....

Here is an example of an acrostic that Britney from New York created.

True words and

Real actions are

Unmistakable

Signs of

Tremendous respect

Britney Maldonado

BUILD YOUR PERSONAL
ABT
TRUST FUND.

Take a good long look at yourself and see what you have done recently to earn your own trust. Complete the following sentences.

I know I can trust myself because I told the truth when:

_____

I know I can trust myself because I kept my promise to:

_____

I know I can trust myself because I followed through on:

_____

I know I can trust myself because I kept a secret when:

_____

I know I can trust myself because I stood up for what I believed was right when I:

_____

Repeat this exercise often. Give yourself credit for being trustworthy whenever you can . . . no matter how big or small the situation or encounter. This is a good way to build trust in yourself. Remember, the more reasons you have to trust yourself, the more your assets grow and the more reasons others will have to put their trust in you. Trust is a powerful asset that makes you a stronger and better person every time you earn it. You're in complete control of your ABT trust fund. How much it grows is up to you.

AB**T**AKES

> **Here's to all the open-minded people.**

A lot of judging goes on at school. People are judged for the clothes they wear, the music they listen to, the way they look, the grades they get, and more. Pretty much everything you do gets judged by someone. But if we could switch our minds to the ABT network, think how much better things could be. We could go from being judgmental to getting along, and popularity wouldn't be an issue. Everyone would see others for their good traits, not their annoying ones or care about how ugly their shirt is. The popular kids judge the unpopular kids, and the unpopular kids judge the popular kids. I still find myself judging others at times and now I catch myself and look at others for their assets first. It really helps me and them.

Bryanne

The best is next.

I START HIGH SCHOOL THIS FALL. AS I LOOK THROUGH MY ABT LENS AT WHAT LIES AHEAD, I SEE MORE RESPONSIBILITY WITH MORE FREEDOM. MY CLASSES WILL BE HARDER AND I WILL FEEL MORE ACCOMPLISHED AS A RESULT OF PASSING THEM. I KNOW I WILL HAVE MORE HOMEWORK, TOO. BUT I THINK DREADING THE WORK IS WORSE THAN DOING THE WORK. WHEN COLLEGES SEE I HAVE TAKEN ACCELERATED COURSEWORK THEY WILL SAY "HE WENT FOR THE CHALLENGE." THAT'S IMPORTANT FOR MY FUTURE. GOING TO HIGH SCHOOL FEELS LIKE A FRESH START. I AM GETTING MORE ORGANIZED AND I'M READY TO WORK HARD. I THINK BEING A GOOD LISTENER WILL HELP ME MAKE FRIENDS. I'M COUNTING ON MY ABILITY TO SOLVE TOUGH PROBLEMS TO PULL ME THROUGH THE HARD TIMES. MY ABTAKE IS THE "BETTER YOU LOOK AT LIFE, THE BETTER IT GETS."

Daniel

CHAPTER 3

CHANGE THE WAY
YOU SEE RELATIONSHIPS
RELATING IS AN
ATTITUDE
AND AN ACTION

RELATIONSHIPS COME IN ALL "SHAPES AND SIZES."

Some relationships are enormously important and form the **INNER CIRCLE** of your life. Your closest and most special relationships fall into this category. Think of the people in your inner circle as the individuals you hope will be in your life forever. The people who form your inner circle are usually members of your family and your best friends. Sometimes teachers, coaches, or neighbors may also be part of your very special inner circle. No matter who makes up your inner circle, it's important for you to recognize who they are, what they mean to you, and to let them know about it as often as you can.

CREATE YOUR OWN PERSONAL UNIVERSE

STEP 1

Think of your inner circle as a group of planets . . . your personal universe with energy and activity (assets) constantly flowing in and out. To create your universe, begin by building your inner circle. Write the names of people you consider to be the most special and important in your life.

(Note: You can add more circles if you want to add more people. Remember, however, only the people who mean the most to you belong in this specific universe!)

STEP 2

Think about what is so great about having each of these people in your life. What you GET and what you GIVE! Here is an example of the "Gives" and "Gets" from some important people in a personal universe.

	WHAT I GIVE	WHAT I GET
My brother	Attention	Support
My best friend	Respect	Respect
My parents	Love	Trust
My cousin	Admiration	Caring
My soccer coach	Extra effort	Recognition

NEXT, FOR EACH PERSON IN YOUR UNIVERSE

STEP 3

Name two or three assets you give and get as you relate to each person. Be specific. Describe what you give to and get from each person in your inner circle. Write the number that corresponds to the assets on the appropriate "I Give" and "I Get" lines.

SAMPLE LIST OF RELATIONSHIP ASSETS:

ASSETS:

1. Attention
2. Admiration
3. Trust
4. Encouragement
5. Guidance
6. Compassion
7. Loyalty
8. Recognition
9. Gratitude
10. Caring
11. Love
12. Support
13. Respect
14. _____
15. _____

Person 1 GIVE/GET

Person 2 GIVE/GET

Person 3 GIVE/GET

(Note: What you give to and get from one person may be identical. Also, you may give or get the same thing from multiple people. That's great!)

WHEN YOU GIVE EVEN MORE THAN YOU GET...

THAT'S THE BEST!

The best relationships are reciprocal. That means you give other people assets they need and you receive assets you need from them. The more you zero in on what you give to and what you get from each relationship, the more you will strengthen that relationship.

The special people in your life are true assets. Without them, you couldn't thrive or even survive. That's why we all need to learn how to make relationships strong and healthy and work hard to keep them that way. Let's take a look at some ways ABT can help do just that.

A TTITUDES
B
+ ACTIONS
= STRONG, HEALTHY RELATIONSHIPS

ABT attitudes and ABT actions are a winning combination when it comes to fostering great relationships. You feel ABT attitudes "inside" of your mind and in your heart. ABT actions involve your visible behavior. ABT attitudes promote ABT actions. By tuning into the ABT network in your mind when you have a conversation with someone, you will automatically zero in on what you like, admire or value about the person. These ABT attitudes will produce a smile on your face, a nod of your head and words that affirm and encourage the other person. People will love to be in your presence.

SEE RESPECT AS JOB 1

The foundation of any healthy relationship is mutual respect. Mutual respect means you value and honor who the other person is as a human being – and that the other person values and honors who you are in the same way. We all have the right to be respected. Along with that right comes an obligation.

You have a right to be respected and you have an obligation to respect others. This "Get and Give" attitude should hold true for all your relationships . . . from people in your inner circle to someone you may have just met. With ABT, this "Get and Give" mindset becomes second nature to you.

For each attitude on the chart below, make a note of the reciprocal action you could take that reflects respect and that makes your respect visible to others. Make sure respect is the first asset you contribute to relationships that are just beginning and to relationships that are continuing to grow. Respect is Job 1.

REFLECT RESPECT

Thoughts and feelings I have when I respect someone . . .	Actions I could take to show respect to someone . . .
That person is worthwhile	_____
That person is interesting	_____
That person is valuable	_____
That person is unique	_____
That person is amazing	_____
That person is incredible	_____
That person is different	_____
That person is surprising	_____

WHO IS ON YOUR MOUNT RUSHMORE?

We build monuments to honor the people we most admire. Monuments are built in all forms, shapes, and dimensions, but mostly we think of them as big and grand. One of the biggest and the grandest is Mount Rushmore in the Black Hills region of South Dakota. Between 1927 and 1941, colossal 60-foot images of four United States presidents were carved into the face of Mount Rushmore to commemorate the first 150 years of American history. George Washington, Thomas Jefferson, Theodore Roosevelt, and Abraham Lincoln were selected to be honored. However, before their images were carved into the mountain, the vision of Mount Rushmore was etched into the creators' minds.

CREATE YOUR ADMIRATION GALLERY

Now it's your turn to celebrate and honor the people you admire, and you don't have to travel to South Dakota to do it. All you need are the Asset-Based Thinking tools that help you spot what is valuable and best about other people first. Asset-Based Thinkers are inspired by discovering admirable qualities in other people, and other people are inspired by the positive feedback they receive from Asset-Based Thinkers.

When you let people know what you see and admire about "who they are" and tell them directly and sincerely, they feel proud of themselves. They put a high value on their relationships with you because you have made the effort to see and celebrate them.

A B Truth

The positive qualities you see in others, you will find in yourself if you just take the time to look.

CREATE YOUR ADMIRATION GALLERY

- Draw a box or picture frame. Then select four people you most admire. Place a photo or drawing of them in the frame.

- Next, list the reason(s) you selected each person. Write about his or her assets (e.g., qualities, skills, and abilities that stand out) and what he or she does that inspires you.

- Finally, make the time to talk with each person and be sure to express your admiration by saying:

"I put you on my Admiration Gallery because _____."
"The assets I admire in you are _____."
"The actions you take that inspire me are _____."

Make sure you notice how enjoyable and rewarding it is for you to celebrate the heroes in your life. It just feels great to give positive feedback to someone you admire. When the other person lights up, you will, too.

Then get ready for a big ABT bonus and wonderful personal "aha" moment. Your bonus is discovering that the qualities you admire in someone else are actually present inside of you as well. How good is that? That is the way ABT works.

Take a look at Matthew's ABT Acrostic. He's from Los Angeles.

A WARENESS

D OES

M AKE YOU HAVE

I NCREDIBLE INSIGHTS INTO

R OLE MODELS YOU WANT TO

E MULATE

Matthew Moor

TRADE PLA

With Asset-Based Thinking, you can learn how to trade places with people and make that skill one of your most powerful assets. You can trade places with people you find interesting and exciting and with people you find frustrating or disappointing. This is how it works. All you have to do is ask yourself this question: "What would I be thinking or feeling if I were acting like that person?" Sure, it's easier to do with someone you view as interesting and exciting. Trading places with someone you see as frustrating and disappointing is definitely harder, but just as worthwhile. **Either way, you benefit and grow.**

THINKABOUTYOUR THINKING

Imagine what a person might be thinking and feeling when:

POSSIBLE THOUGHTS AND FEELINGS

Scoring points in a game

Winning an argument

Standing up for a friend

Making a great entrance

Fixing a problem

Learning a new skill

Giving the right answer in class

Getting an A in math

Now imagine what a person might be thinking and feeling when:

POSSIBLE THOUGHTS AND FEELINGS

Bullying someone less popular

Interrupting your conversation

Cutting in line

Yelling at you

Spreading gossip

Telling a lie

Getting in someone's face

Ignoring you

BE BRAVE

BE BOLD

When someone hurts your feelings, what do you say and how do you react? You might retaliate with statements such as "Get off my case!", "Get out of my face!" or "Whatever!" You might storm out of a room or pout or kick the dirt to let off some steam. Although retaliation in words or with an action is common, it does nothing to improve the situation or the relationship. In fact, it almost always makes things worse.

ABT offers alternative ways of handling minor spats, communication breakdowns and stressful interactions.

TELL THE TRUTH

TURN THINGS AROUND

ABT gives you a chance to turn things around, and simultaneously get the message across about how you feel. It is often difficult to stand up for yourself. Sometimes it takes courage and conviction to bring up sensitive subjects. You might hesitate or shy away from expressing how you feel or declare your position if you think it will cause more conflict or make matters worse. Most of the time, if you are brave enough to speak your truth in a clear, neutral way, your honesty is welcomed. Let's look at two ways to be brave and bold enough to tell the truth.

TRY THIS

SAY "AVOCADO"

Some teens have adopted the word "avocado" as a code word for "My feelings just got hurt" or "I am really sensitive about that" or "Hey, wait just a second . . . you've gone too far." It is your "inner circle" safety valve. So, in the middle of a conversation or interaction, when you or another person says "avocado," there's an instant awareness that something said or done has struck a negative chord. You have to be prepared to both speak and hear "avocado" – it's a two-way street. When you say or hear "avocado," it is instantly understood that something is wrong, feelings are hurt, feathers are ruffled, and that apologies and remedial actions are needed.

It doesn't really matter which word you choose as your code word for "ouch" as long as it's a neutral one. Be creative and select your own code word. Something like "shoelace," "popcorn," "baseball," or "sidewalk" could be the code word between you and your close friends. Any word will work as long as it prompts a time-out rather than sounding an alarm.

GET BACK ON TRACK: The ABT principle here is to signal "ouch" without sounding too mad, too hurt, or too sensitive. By voicing a neutral code word, no one gets defensive or fights back. Both people feel better.

WHEN AN "AVOCADO" ISN'T ENOUGH... HAVE COURAGEOUS CONVERSATIONS

Sometimes altercations are major (not minor) and really have the potential of severely disrupting a relationship. For example, you or someone else may tell a lie, or spread hurtful gossip, or intentionally bully the other person. In these instances, you need more than a code word to repair and restart. For these bigger relationship breakdowns, you can use an ABT power tool called Courageous Conversations. Being brave and bold in response to bigger breakdowns is especially important to building trust in the long run. No one wants to lie or be lied to. Telling the truth when it's hard to do is a skill worth building.

STEP 1: COMMIT TO ADMIT:

Ask yourself what you may have done to contribute to the problem or breakdown in the relationship. Maybe you ignored the other person or have done something that upset, frustrated, angered, or hurt the other person. Think hard about the part you may have played, whether intentionally or by accident. Admit your part and apologize.

STEP 2 : THINK BACK TO MOVE AHEAD:

Think about what you like about the other person. Name 5 qualities or abilities you admire. Remember times you have had fun or have enjoyed and appreciated being with that person. Maybe you are great baseball fans and go to games together. Maybe you are hiking buddies. Maybe you took ballet lessons or learned to camp together. This step helps you shine a true positive light on the person.

(Note: You may feel so much better after doing steps 1 and 2 that you can stop here and just forgive the person and see what happens. However, if you still feel the need to work things out, be brave enough to complete the next steps.)

STEP 3:
MAKE TIME STOP!

Set up a time to have a 10-to-15 minute conversation without being interrupted. Before you meet the other person, be sure to prepare what you will say and how you will say it. Remind yourself why you like the person. **Rehearse your opening comments using this sequence:**

A) Open on a positive and clear note. Say something like this: "I want to talk to you about something very important – our friendship." (Put this sentence in your own words. Say it just as <u>you</u> would say it.)

B) Tell the Truth: "When you (state what the person did or said here), then I feel (state your feelings here)."

C) "I want to work this out. Would you be willing to talk to me about what happened so we can (state your goal here)?"

D) Now let the person respond to your request. Most of the time people will say yes and will talk things out with you. If so, let the conversation take its course. Now it's important for you to be a good listener and take in the other person's reasons and feelings. Your goal is to get the relationship back on track – not worrying about being right or proving how wrong the other person has been. **Personal relationships built on mutual respect are positive and resilient. They stand the test of time and can be repaired with equal doses of ABT & TLC.**

KNOCK SOMEONE'S Socks off

There are different types of surprises that knock your socks off. Some are tangible (things you can see and touch), such as new clothes, music, books, or games. Often the best surprises show up in the form of your favorite experiences, such as going to a live concert, hiking in the woods, eating cookie-dough ice cream, or having a slumber party. Sometimes people really surprise you by what they do, such as helping with your homework, cleaning your room, running errands for you, or cooking your favorite meal.

Don't you just love a surprise that totally blows you away? Something or someone that breaks the monotony of day-to-day routines, with a big "wow" factor that makes you smile, laugh, and celebrate? Asset-Based Thinkers both create and experience these "knock your socks off moments" as an important part of their life. When somebody gives you an amazing, positively mind-blowing experience, you are thankful. You appreciate that person's effort. **You feel special.**

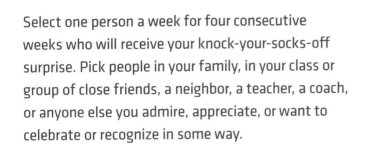

Select one person a week for four consecutive weeks who will receive your knock-your-socks-off surprise. Pick people in your family, in your class or group of close friends, a neighbor, a teacher, a coach, or anyone else you admire, appreciate, or want to celebrate or recognize in some way.

For each person, think about the impact and emotional nature of the knock-your-socks-off moment you want to create. Try to see it and "be there." Then specify the type of surprise you want to give: a gift, an experience, or a helpful action. You may also want to pick a particular time and day that can take the "wow" factor to an even higher level and REALLY knock their socks off. After all, timing is everything, right?

KNOCK SOMEBODY'S SOCKS OFF

Use this chart to help you make your plan. Look at the plan that Nadia made as an example.

ABT SURPRISES
WHO WILL YOU SURPRISE?

WHAT WILL YOU GIVE?
GIFT, EXPERIENCE, HELPFUL ACTION

W1 _____

E2 _____

E3 _____

K4 _____

ABT Surprises	Who will you surprise:	What will you give?	When will you do this ?	WOW – what impact will you have?
WEEK 1	My mom	Clean my closet	Monday after school	She will not believe it!
WEEK 2	Angelina (my best friend)	Make her a bracelet	Saturday morning	She will know how much I like her.
WEEK 3	Mama	Do the dishes after dinner	Tuesday evening	She will be so shocked!
WEEK 4	My grandfather	Plant tomatoes in the garden	Sunday afternoon	He will love to see me help.

WHEN WILL YOU DO THIS?
(MORNING, AFTERNOON, EVENING)

WOW – WHAT IMPACT WILL YOU HAVE?

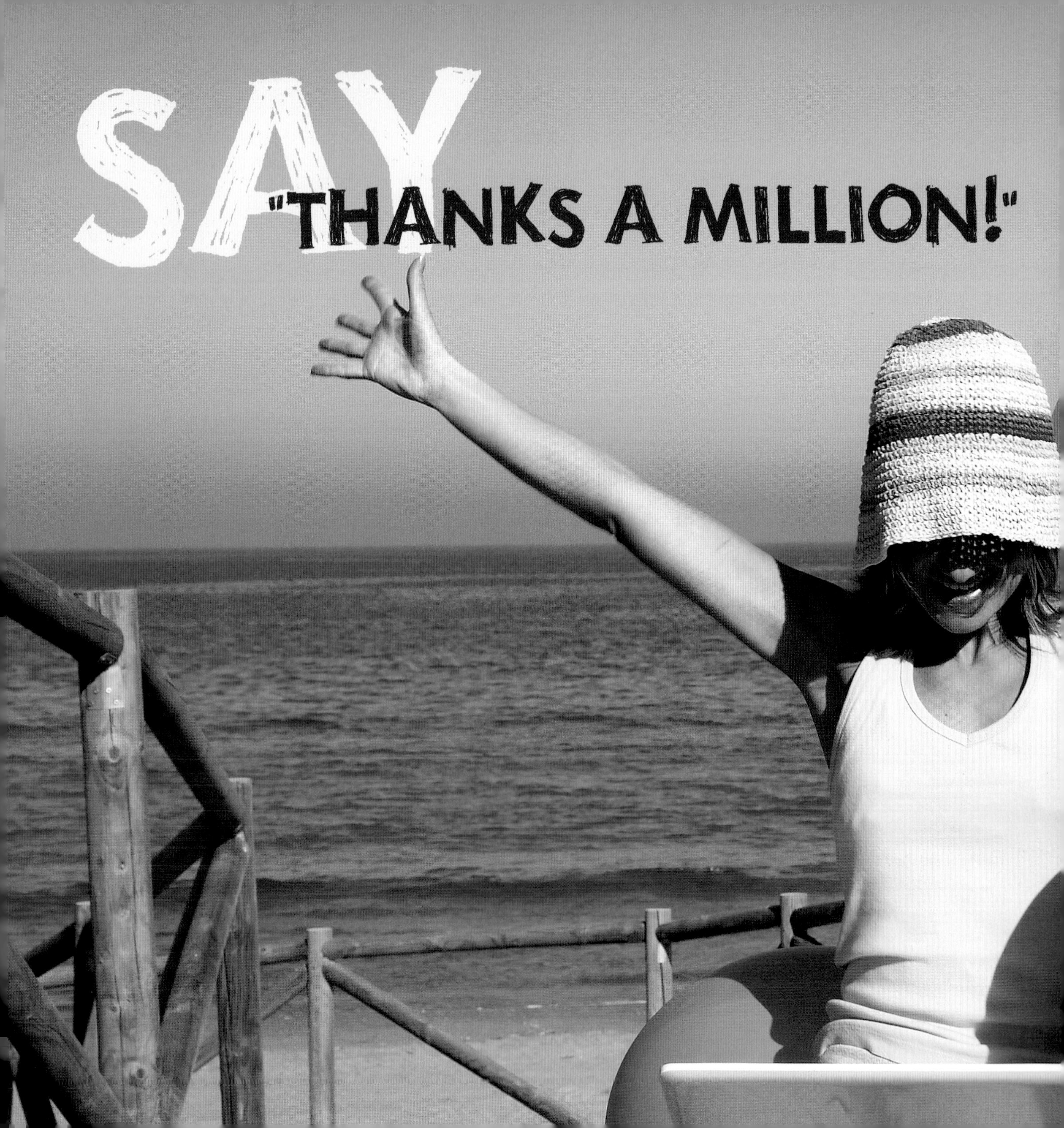
SAY "THANKS A MILLION!"

The phrase "thanks a million" expresses deep appreciation for what someone else does or says. It means that if we could say "thank you" a million times, we would. We learn to say "thank you" as very young children. Our parents teach us to say "thanks" because it's the polite thing to do. It's a phrase and a sentiment that exists in every language and culture.

Pretty soon, saying "thank you" becomes an almost automatic response whenever anyone does something nice or helpful such as opening the door, passing the dessert, or doing a favor for us. The most incredible thing about such a simple phrase is that it can be so much more than an expression of politeness. You can use it as a powerful asset to make your relationships stronger, yourself happier and healthier, and positively impact pretty much everything you do.

40 WAYS TO SAY "THANKS A MILLION"

Review the following 40 possible reasons why you want to thank someone.
Pick a word from the list or select your own that specifies why you are grateful.

SUPPORTING

BEING CARING PROTECTING REVEALING

REWARDING TALKING REMEMBERING DOING SHOWING

RECOGNIZING THINKING STOPPING GIVING PREVENTING BRINGING

RESPECTING THINKING STOPPING GIVING PREVENTING SAYING

FINDING BELIEVING SHARING DEVELOPING CELEBRATING

KEEPING FINISHING DEMONSTRATING SENDING COMMITTING

HOLDING BUILDING REPAIRING SURPRISING BUYING

HELPING RESOLVING OFFERING GUIDING TRYING PROVIDING

FEELING

1. "Thank you for _____." (specify action)

2. "This made me feel _____"
   (express your positive reaction)

3. "This was important to me because _____"
   (express the overall impact)

Try handwriting a note that includes all three of the above elements in your thank-you message. A handwritten note will stand out because so much communication is by e-mail or text messages. To make your thank you even more outstanding, deliver the note in person. Don't forget you can embellish it with illustrations, stickers, or anything else that celebrates the person you are thanking.

A CALL OUT FROM:

Mike Venezia

ABTO: My cousin Matt and his big shoulders

I really enjoy sports, especially baseball and lacrosse, and I love playing video games. When summer vacation rolls around, that's just about all I want to do. I didn't think much about it until this past February when my cousin Matt did something very cool. Matt is 17 and an even bigger sports fan and gamer than I am. He decided that he would give up sports and video games during his winter break from school and go with a group of teens to Nicaragua to build houses for the poor. Matt helped me realize that sometimes giving up things can be a good thing, especially when it comes to helping others. When I get old enough I hope to follow Matt's example. Thanks, cuz. You're a winner!

A CALL OUT FROM

ABTO: Ezra — an inspiration

LuCaS WASIAK

My friend Ezra has cerebral palsy and is confined to a wheelchair. But that doesn't stop him from being in an "up" mood and part of the action with all the rest of us. Ez loves and lives baseball, like me. He makes up for what he can't do physically by going to games and talking baseball like a pro. He's studied the stats and knows more about teams and players than just about anyone. And it doesn't stop at baseball. He even went to the paintball park and mixed it up with all of us. Way to go, Ez. You're amazing!

(Now it's time to look at your responsibilities through the ABT lens. Asset-Based Thinking will help you shift from feeling that "I have to" to feeling that "I want to.")

CHAPTER 4
CHANGE THE WAY YOU SEE RESPONSIBILITIES:
HOW THINGS TURN OUT DEPENDS ON HOW YOU TUNE IN

A BRAND-NEW DAY.
EVERY DAY!

Each and every day is a new start. It could be full of possibilities and opportunities, or it could be fraught with problems and challenges. What happens to you can be good – even great. What happens can be bad – even horrible. Hans Selye, a world-renowned physiologist known as the "Father of Stress Research," once said, "It's not what happens to you that matters, it's how you react that counts." **Tuning in to the ABT network in your mind can make all the difference in how your day turns out.**

What Dr. Selye said is true. For example, when it comes to positive events and experiences, you could just take them in stride as the normal course of your day OR you could use ABT to "supercharge" them and make the most of what they have to offer. ABT helps you get the most out of good fortune and hard-won victories, such as winning a game, being chosen for the play, going to a great party, reading an exciting book, or getting all your math problems correct. In each case, when you focus your attention on celebrating yourself, others who chipped in, and the actual outcome, you add a whole new dimension. When you reflect on the steps you took to reach your goal, you discover what you learned along the way.

A = ATTITUDE OF GRATITUDE

B = BEATS COMPLAINING EVERY

T = TIME

With Asset-Based Thinking, you look at each opportunity and possibility with a refreshing and energizing attitude. You realize that most good things that happen are a mixture of personal effort, making the most of circumstances and good luck. You give yourself and others credit where credit is due, you make the most of the assets around you, and you appreciate the part that good fortune had to play. **Being grateful** for all the things that happen **builds confidence** in yourself and in the fact that **the universe is indeed "a friendly place."**

FRIEND OR FOE

Albert Einstein once said that it is each person's responsibility to decide if the universe is a friendly or unfriendly place. ABT helps you see that your world is, more often than not, a "friend" offering enormous potential and possibilities just waiting to be recognized and realized by you. The more opportunities you look for, the better chance you have of seizing them and making many great things happen.

SEE THROUGH THE SETBACKS

When it comes to dealing with disappointments and setbacks, ABT can pave the way and help make the road a lot less rocky and risky. First, ABT helps you face and deal with these negative events. Then you are ready to look through and beyond them to actually make the most of problems and challenges, mistakes and mishaps. The good news is that most of the same ABT principles apply to both unpleasant and pleasant circumstances. So, it's just a matter of getting out your "remote" and tuning in to the ABT network in your mind. When something bad happens, ABT equips you with the tools to see the gains and benefits hidden inside your negative circumstances. No matter how bad they might seem at first, when you look deeper and harder through your ABT lens, you will find benefits.

With Asset-Based Thinking, you look beyond the immediate negative event toward what you can get out of it in the long run. Asset-Based Thinkers ask themselves questions such as: "What did this loss or mistake teach me that makes me smarter or more real?" or "How could I turn this problem into a chance to know myself better or to ask others for help, or learn a new skill or respect myself more by how I deal with it?"

With ABT, you learn to milk problems for all they are worth. You get engaged instead of being enraged. You understand and respect the losses AND you are determined to make your troubles yield gains. You look at the "bad news" courageously and honestly. You put your comfort and pride on the sidelines for as long as it takes you to see just how you can **use the problem to your own advantage.**

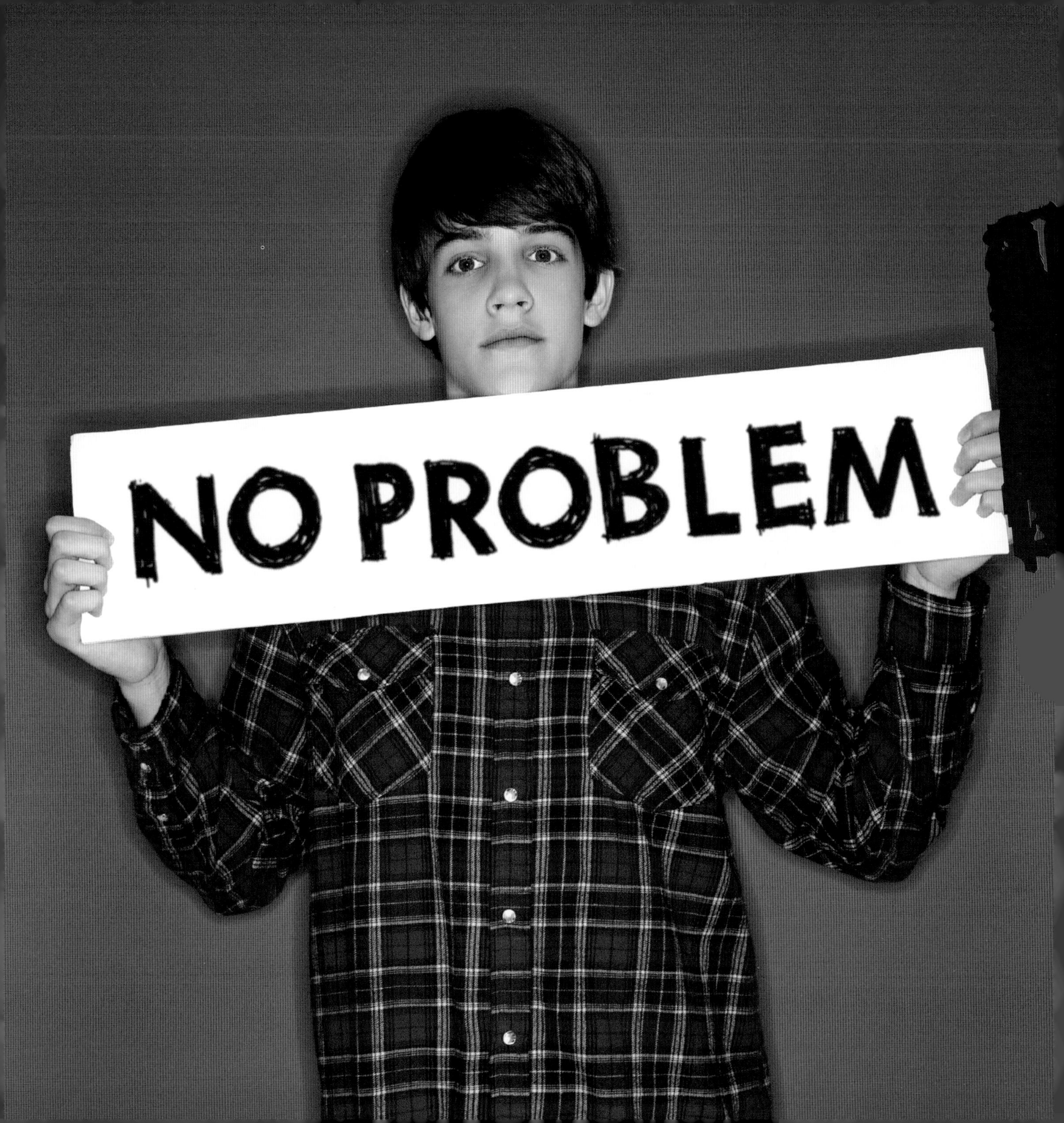
NO PROBLEM

GET LUCKY

Asset-Based Thinkers know that things don't always work out perfectly or as planned. They know that life isn't always fair — that sometimes it's just a matter of luck.

luck(n) "Something that happens by chance rather than as a logical consequence . . . the arbitrary distribution of events or outcomes"

ASSET-BASED THINKERS understand that luck can go both ways . . . "good" luck or "bad" luck. Bad luck is not something anyone welcomes. With ABT, while you don't necessarily like what happens, you are willing to learn and grow from it. In the face of adversity of all kinds, ABT gives you the chance to become more resilient, a more creative problem-solver, and more inspiring to yourself and others. ABT puts you in charge, not of what happens but of how you deal with what happens.

RESPONSIBILITIES

The title of this part of the book is "Change the Way You See Responsibilities." If you look closely at the word *responsibility*, you can see that its root is made up of two words — *response* plus *ability*. When you break the word *responsibility* into its two components, you get a new view of what it means. From this dual vantage point, responsibility means the "ability to respond."

RESPONSE + ABILITY

RESPONSIBLE

Think about that for a moment. When you are responsible, you are able to respond. With ABT, you are able to respond to whatever happens in positive ways that benefit you and other people. Life doesn't get any better than that! Let this part of the book help you take your ability to respond to the next level.

ABLE TO RESPOND

FOR YOUR SAFETY
lease Swim in Front of Lifeguard

Lifeguards on Duty
10:00am - 5:00pm weekdays
10:00am - 5:30pm weekends & holidays

Most people love to have choices and options for most things in their life. For example, when it comes to the clothes you wear, the food you eat, the friends you hang out with, or the time and place you do your homework, it feels good to be able to make the decisions about what, who, when, and where. Making good decisions about your options is a skill you keep developing over time. The ability to make good decisions that serve you well over the short and long term is extremely valuable. Making good decisions will lead to a stronger, healthier, happier you.

DECISIONS, DECISIONS, DECISIONS...

ABT
ASSESSMENT

Every day, you make many different types of decisions and you know firsthand that sometimes it can be difficult to determine which choice is best. When you feel upset or stressed about a decision, ABT can really help you out. With only a small investment of ABT effort, you can improve the quality of your decisions and your life dramatically. As a bonus, ABT assessments can transform making your best decisions into a fun and exciting experience.

In ABT workshops, we turned the decision-making process into a challenging game. This set the stage for learning how to weigh the merits of choices that are sometimes difficult to make.

The next exercise shows you how to put this **ABT ASSESSMENT** tool to work.

ASSESS YOUR OPTIONS...
MAKE YOUR CHOICE

STEP 1

Listed below are some typical dilemmas that the teens in our workshops encountered. Notice that each dilemma can be resolved in one of two ways. Read each dilemma and consider whether you agree with the resolution that is presented. If you agree, check the "Deal" box. If you don't agree, check the "No Deal" box. Then write the reasons for your particular decision. You will quickly see that the better your reasons, the better your decision will be for you and everyone involved.

DILEMMAS WITH RESOLUTIONS

You have a ton of extra homework and you're not sure how you will get it all done. Your favorite show is on at 7 p.m. but when 7 p.m. rolls around, you're not even halfway done. You take a break to watch your show.

DEAL ◯ **NO DEAL** ◯

You love wearing comfy jeans and T-shirts. You don't really care about brand names and know they cost a lot more. But name brands sure seem to matter to other people in your circle of friends. You stick with what you're comfortable with even if they tease you.

DEAL ◯ **NO DEAL** ◯

There is a new girl in school and she's sitting alone in the lunchroom. Your friends don't seem to notice or care that she's there but you feel bad for her. If you were the new kid, you'd want people to notice you. You invite her to sit with you.

DEAL ◯ **NO DEAL** ◯

You have been friends with your neighbor since you were 3. You've been noticing lately that she is being picked on at school more and more. Your other friends tease you about her being so uncool. You defend your friend and continue hanging out with her.

DEAL ◯ **NO DEAL** ◯

You have been sick off and on all week. Your parents said you can play in your soccer game on Saturday only if you're well by Friday. You REALLY want to play. On Friday morning you wake up and still feel pretty crummy. Instead of telling the truth, you say you're feeling fine so that you can play Saturday.

DEAL ◯ **NO DEAL** ◯

MY REASONS WHY

_____

_____

_____

_____

_____

THE DECISION: "TUG oF

Sometimes you will make decisions based only on your self-interests and what feels best for you. That's okay, as long as it doesn't harm other people. Other times you will find that the decision you make (or you know you ought to make) isn't the one that makes you happiest. Maybe it makes your mom or your brother or a friend happy instead. As long as it doesn't harm you, that's okay, too. Or maybe you just sense that, in the long run, a decision that seems less thrilling now (or that doesn't give you the "short run" result you want) will end up being the best one or have the greatest long-term benefit. That's okay, too. Really.

THE RIGHT BALANCE:

Basically, it will probably take you a big part of your life to balance it all out and figure out how to weigh the costs, benefits, and possible consequences of all of your decisions (big and small). ABT can help you arrive at the "right" one with the greatest benefit to you and the people around you faster and with more confidence and conviction. Sure, you won't always get it right, but the first step in getting it right more often than not is being more aware of and careful about how you make your decisions.

sTReSS:
HEADS oR TAILS, IT'S YOUR CALL

Like a coin, stressful adversity has two sides simultaneously— the upside and the downside. The upside offers you new possibilities and potential. The downside presents problems and dangers. In fact, the Chinese language has one symbol for the word *crisis* that means both "danger" and "opportunity."

ABT

ADVERSITY

Whether minor or major, adversity can help you or hurt you, depending upon how you SEE it. Seeing adversity through your ABT lens helps you do two things.

1. **FOCUS AND DIRECT** most of your attention on the positive side of what adversity has to offer.

2. **LET GO** of the worry and anxiety that adversity can trigger.

TURN STRESS INTO SUCCESS: The best way to develop ABT skills for turning stress into success is to role-play and project yourself into potentially stressful situations. Then apply ABT stress skills to each type of adversity and watch what happens.

TRY THIS

ABT STRESS BUSTER

Put a check mark next to the three sources of adversity that stress you out.

SOURCES OF STRESS:

_____ HAVING TOO MUCH HOMEWORK

_____ ARGUING WITH PARENTS

_____ BEING LATE

_____ FEELING REJECTED BY FRIENDS

_____ LOSING THE GAME

_____ MISSING DEADLINES

_____ MAKING MISTAKES

_____ FAILING A TEST

_____ BEING EMBARRASSED OR HUMILIATED

_____ ANOTHER SOURCE OF ADVERSITY: _____

Whenever you encounter any one of your sources of adversity, use the following ABT STRESS-BUSTING STRATEGY.

LET GO OF YOUR FEAR

When you are faced with a particularly high stress level or feeling overwhelmed by adversity, use this ABT visualization technique. Picture your bad feelings – anger, stress, worry, and anxiety – as a big red balloon. Picture yourself blowing up the balloon, bigger and bigger with each deep breath you inhale and then exhale. Every breath is getting those bad feelings out of you and into this big red balloon. Keep going until in your mind's eye you actually can see the balloon get so big, so full of everything you're feeling, that it might explode. Then just let it go.

GRAB HOLD OF YOUR UPSIDE

Now, with your fear pushed aside, you can ask yourself ABT questions that will open up new ways for you to SEE the adversity. "What are the possibilities and opportunities for growing and learning, for becoming wiser, stronger, healthier, more loving, and productive? What is the personal upside of this adversity?"

GO FOR IT – TAKE ACTION STEP 3

The opportunities and possibilities that you see in the upside will help you identify the steps you will take to overcome the adversity and reap the benefits. Here's a tried-and-true ABT tool to help you do just that.

Deficit-Based Thinking (DBT) creates internal turmoil that leads to frustration and dissatisfaction. When you focus on the negative, your attitude and personality reflect it. You mope around feeling upset, uncomfortable, and restless.

Let's look at a common situation that often triggers DBT and see how ABT can help you shift. Have you ever compared yourself to someone who has more than you . . . more clothes, more talent, more freedom, more friends, or more athletic skill? Comparing yourself to others you believe are more fortunate than you may be a common practice, but it also is a very risky proposition. First it leads to jealousy, then to negative critical feelings about yourself and how inadequate you are.

WHAT YOU HAVE IS "JUST ENOUGH"

I'M NOT

Self-criticism hurts and damages when you give yourself negative "not enough" messages. They can arise from different sources and come at you from many directions. It can come from comparing yourself to other teens you know, a brother, sister, or cousin, comparing yourself to famous people in music, on TV, or in the movies. Sometimes others just seem better off than you are. "Not enough" is a DBT attitude and phrase that definitely leads to big-time dissatisfaction with yourself and your circumstances. So, tell yourself that you've had enough of not enough! Watch what happens.

ENOUGH WITH NOT ENOUGH!

ATTRACTIVE ENOUGH

SMART ENOUGH

POPULAR ENOUGH

RICH ENOUGH

TALENTED ENOUGH

LET YOU SHINE THROUGH.

Asset-Based Thinking can lead your way out of a DBT day.

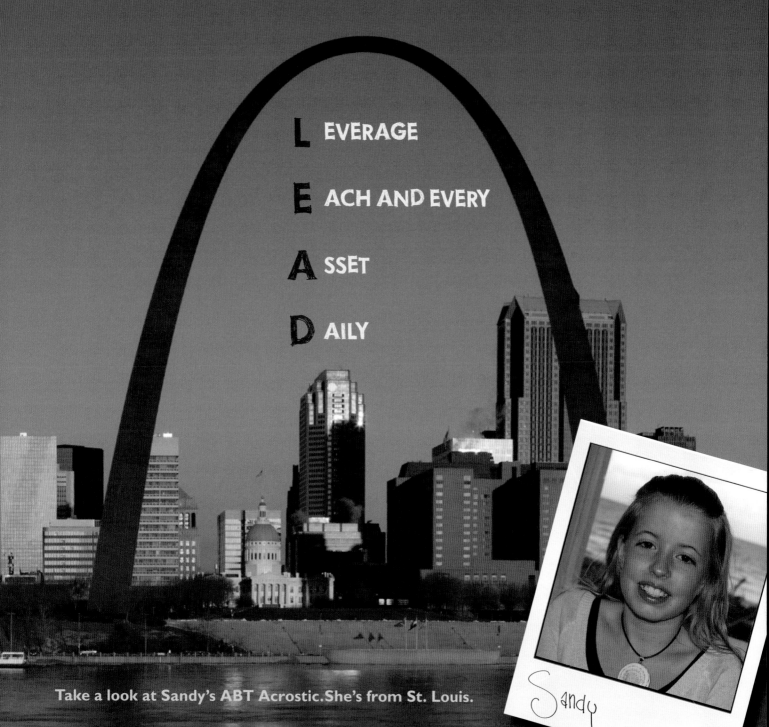

L EVERAGE

E ACH AND EVERY

A SSET

D AILY

Take a look at Sandy's ABT Acrostic. She's from St. Louis.

Sandy

ELIZABETH

SPEAK WITH

SUBSTANCE SIZZLE SOUL

YOU'RE IN CHARGE

When you change the way you see responsibility, you realize that sometimes it is YOUR responsibility to speak up for yourself, take a stand for what you believe in and be the champion for the opinions and rights of others. Speaking up, speaking out, and standing tall are ABT skills you can develop right now that will be valuable assets for the rest of your life. **Focus on The S Factors . . . three assets essential to high-impact communication. Substance, Sizzle and Soul**

With Asset-Based Thinking, you can make sure any message you deliver has as much impact and effectiveness as the most influential and effective leaders you have ever seen, heard, or read about. The best way to see how the ABT approach to high-impact communication works is to reflect on some important questions.

Who are the most effective and influential leaders? Think of the most charismatic, amazing, and inspirational public figures in history. What made them so powerful, so important, and so irresistible? What did they have that we all want? It's simple: **Passion. Sincerity. Pizzazz.** People believed in their messages and the messenger. All effective speakers and leaders know exactly what to do to inspire others to follow and to take action.

BELIEVE IN SOMETHING BIG.

Just believing in a mighty cause – something big that can change the world for the better – advances that cause in powerful ways. Your belief and commitment can make the difference between success and failure, progress and setback, victory or defeat.

With ABT, you can learn to expand your perspective beyond the immediate opportunities, possibilities and challenges of your everyday world. Let ABT show you how to get behind Big Ideas that benefit you, your inner circle, and the wider world all at one time. Let ABT set your sights on what you have to contribute, what you want to make happen and on leading and inspiring others in bigger and wider ways.

When you Believe in Something Big, life becomes an adventure of your own making. You put yourself in the driver's seat. You decide the destinations. You learn to use surprise, serendipity, and even setbacks to make your adventure more interesting and more worthwhile. You gain confidence and belief in who you are, where you are going and how to get there.

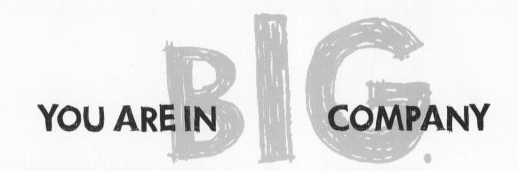

YOU ARE IN BIG COMPANY

There are countless inspiring examples of teens like you who have dared to Believe in Something Big and, as a result, have changed themselves and the world for the better. Every year since 2004, Build-A-Bear Workshop® searches for and selects what they call Huggable Heroes.® Huggable Heroes are "young leaders who are an inspiration to all around them because of the positive difference they have been able to make in their neighborhoods, schools, communities, and the wider world."

Four Build-A-Bear Workshop Huggable Heroes participated in ABT interviews so they could share their stories, advice, and insights with you. As you read their stories and comments, notice what attracts you, inspires you, and what you admire most. **Remember this ABT TRUTH: The assets you see in someone else — you have inside of yourself.** These ABT role models can get you started in Believing in YOUR Something Big. Enjoy.

HUGGABLE HEROES®

Honored By Build-A-Bear Workshop®

WHO ARE THEY?

A Build-A-Bear Workshop Huggable Hero
is a young person 18 years of age or under
doing awesome stuff to make a difference
in his or her neighborhood, school,
community or around the world.

SUITCASES FOR KIDS

What would you be thinking and feeling if you heard story after story about what life is like for the foster children who not only have to move frequently but also have to carry their clothes and other belongings in black garbage bags?

In a recent ABT interview, Welland (now age 19) answered that very question. He said, "I was 6 years old and my sister Aubyn was 8 when we first heard stories about foster children. Leslie, my older sister, was a social worker who made sure the children moved safely to their new foster homes. Aubyn and I were scared by Leslie's stories. We talked about how hard it would be if we had to move from home to home. Both of us were really upset by the fact that the kids had nothing to carry their clothes in except trash bags. We thought the foster children must feel like garbage themselves."

Welland continues, "Then one day, somehow we moved past talking about the problem to brainstorming what we could do to provide the foster children with some dignity and self-respect when they moved. Leslie had been asking my mom if she had any old suitcases in the attic that she could donate to the foster children. My mom was sympathetic but had only one or two to give away. Suddenly, Aubyn and I got the idea that we might be able to get more luggage from people who had some to spare for a good cause. At that moment we decided to take action and do something. We said, "Hey, we should start a project to collect suitcases for the foster children!"

"We named our project Suitcases For Kids. We posted flyers at grocery stores, community buildings, and libraries. We spoke to schools, churches, and civic groups. We put out drop-off boxes around town. Aubyn and I asked 4-H Clubs, Girl Scout and Boy Scout troops, and our friends to help us. Every day we begged our mom to drive us around to check on how many suitcases had been donated. We made our rounds every day for two weeks. No suitcases showed up—not one! We were very discouraged; this was our lowest point. We were disappointed and thought people did not want to help. We thought our idea would not be successful."

"My mom felt sorry, too. She said, 'You two have worked so hard and put in a lot of effort. So I'm going to the thrift store and buy all the suitcases they have to sell.' This ended up being about 30. We were grateful for her support but still felt disheartened that we did not achieve our goal of 300 suitcases, enough for a suitcase for every foster child in our county."

"The next day a strange thing happened. Our mom took us to pick up the drop-off boxes and the suitcases had started to roll in. In less than a month, we delivered 375 suitcases to the Department of Social Services. We could not believe it! It was amazing to see the piles of suitcases coming in. Soon we didn't have enough room to store them. Our living room began filling up. A local builder donated a storage shed for our backyard. We were surprised and excited about the growth and support of our appeal."

"Our idea spread like wildfire with the support of countless volunteers and many corporate sponsorships. At the end of our first year, Suitcases For Kids had chapters in 19 states. At the end of our second year, we stopped counting suitcases after we had collected over 25,000. Our nonprofit had expanded to have chapters in all 50 states and Canada. Today, 13 years later, Aubyn remains CEO and I am the president of Suitcases For Kids, which is currently active in 93 countries."

BELIEVE IN SOMETHING BIG.

Welland's ABT Insights and Advice:

• When you give 100% to whatever you believe in, you are more likely to make it happen AND it makes you feel great!

• One person can make a difference by standing up for an idea and leading by example, which inspires individuals to become active, productive citizens who are dedicated to community service.

• If you give others a chance to support you, most people will join in if you make them aware of your cause and show them how to help because people of all ages like sharing their time, energy, and resources.

• When things get challenging, take the time to search within yourself and think about your ideas. Ask yourself, "Why am I doing this?" That's how you'll discover what you are made of and how you will become motivated to make positive changes and improvements in yourself and in your world.

"Aubyn and I have changed the way we see ourselves. Instead of thinking of ourselves as young children not old enough to organize a project, we realize that we were visionaries who had a dream to help children. We developed into leaders who continue to inspire volunteers of all ages who share a common goal of community service. We have made a lifelong commitment to helping those in need. We have a motto — live to give!"

www.suitcasesforkids.org

HUGGABLE HEROES

Welland is a 2006 Build-A-Bear Workshop Huggable Hero

THE LITTLE RED WAGON FOUNDATION

Making a difference for other people often starts with meeting their basic needs for health and well-being. At age 10, Zach from Florida founded a not-for-profit organization called the Little Red Wagon Foundation, so that he could help people on his own terms. He wanted the power to set his own agenda and priorities without compromising the contributions he believed to be the most important. In a recent ABT interview, Zach explained, "There are many organizations that have a mission to provide for the basic survival support for people in need. I could have joined forces with one of them, but then I would have to stick to their mission only. I want to do more."

"I believe it is important to do something special for kids, to go beyond the basics, to show that you know and care about them as kids. So, for example, when the Little Red Wagon Foundation prepares backpacks for children who are victims of natural disasters (such as hurricanes, floods, tornadoes, or wildfires), we include a toy, a book, and some candy along with food, first-aid kits, water, and other basics. These extra items communicate that fun and play and enjoying yourself are part of taking care of yourself and getting back to normal."

"I got interested in helping people after Hurricane Charlie. I was six years old then and didn't really understand anything about volunteerism or community service – I just wanted to help. Now I believe that making a difference for others is an indescribably great experience, whether you are my age (10) or older or younger."

"My goal is to raise one million dollars for kids in need. I walked from Tampa to Tallahassee (280 miles) to raise awareness and money for homeless kids. This year I am walking from Tallahassee to Atlanta to raise money to build a new home with Habitat for Humanity for a homeless family."

"When I first started my walkathons, people thought it was a joke. Then the national news picked up the story. It was covered on NBC, FOX, and CNN. Then the local news broadcast the story, too. Finally, people realized I was, and am, serious."

LITTLE RED WAGON FOUNDATION, INC.
Kids Helping Kids
One Wagon Full At A Time!

zachary

BELIEVE IN SOMETHING BIG.

HUGGABLE HEROES
Zach is a 2007 Build-A-Bear Workshop Huggable Hero

Zach's ABT Insights and Advice:

• Pick a cause and then just start doing something. If you plan and think too much, you lose confidence.

• Anyone can rally people and be a champion if his or her heart is in the right place.

• No one can make you do anything — it has to be your own idea and you have to be committed.

www.littleredwagonfoundation.com

HOOps OF HOPE

Life can be difficult — sometimes very difficult. When a person you love gets sick or dies, it's natural to be sad, to feel pain and grief, to feel angry and lonely. In the spring of 2004, a boy named Austin (who was 9 years old at the time) felt sad and hurt after watching a video of children in Zambia whose parents had died of AIDS. Austin was growing up in Phoenix, Arizona, a world away from Zambia. But he still identified with the painful suffering of the children there.

In his ABT interview, Austin reflected on just how incredibly sad he felt when he saw children who no longer had their parents, and sometimes not even relatives, to live with. "I remember thinking to myself that, except for being orphans, these kids were exactly like me. That's when I decided I had to do something to help."

"So, on World AIDS Day in 2004, I had people sponsor me to raise money while doing something that I knew how to do and would do some good. Shooting baskets. I shot 2,057 free throws to represent the 2,057 kids who would be orphaned in just one day in Zambia. We raised almost $3,000. I sent the money to World Vision, an organization that helps AIDS orphans get access to food, clothing, shelter, school, and now a medical testing facility."

"Hoops of Hope was born and thousands of people have joined in basketball shoot-a-thons we call Hoops of Hope. Aside from raising money, to me there is something very special about seeing a ball rise high in the air and then hearing the swoosh it makes when it lands in the basket. And what is really amazing is that Hoops of Hope participants have raised over $400,000 to date."

"The money has built a medical lab for medical staff who test parents for HIV/AIDS and then administer medicine that prolongs their lives. I am proud of what we have been able to accomplish — but not surprised. Kids love to make a difference when they are given a chance. They will blow you away with what they make happen. They are not as influenced by the negative points of view of the adult world. They don't wonder so much about how and why parents get AIDS in the first place. We don't think about anything but helping to prevent and cure the problem. Some adults believe AIDS is a punishment for doing something bad. Kids just don't think like that."

Now, at age 14, Austin thinks the Hoops of Hope experience has made a big positive difference in his life, too. He said, "I have more self-confidence now than I did before. My self-confidence helps me push through barriers because I know deep inside I can do it. Helping people gives me an awesome feeling of happiness and joy. When you make positive changes for someone else, it changes you, too. I am more grateful. I am more goal-oriented. I now know my purpose in life. I know where I am going. I want a career in public policy or politics so I can help lead this country out of the trouble it's in."

BELIEVE IN SOMETHING BIG.

HUGGABLE HEROES

Austin is a 2008 Build-A-Bear Workshop Huggable Hero

Austin's ABT Insights and Advice:

• If you aim high, you get high (if you aim low, you get low). The bigger your goal, the more you excel.

• The best way to know if you are a leader is to look behind you to see if anyone is following you.

• If you keep trying to make a difference, if you stick with it, it will be contagious.

www.hoopsofhope.org

RANDOMKID

RandomKid is a unique 501(C)3 nonprofit organization that brings kids together from around the globe to solve real-world problems. Talia founded RandomKid with an adult partner in 2005 when she was 10 years old. Now 13, Talia works with any random kid who wants to turn compassion into action. "RandomKid helps kids help others," Talia said, "and one of the best things about it is seeing kids' faces – both the givers and recipients – as they celebrate the results together."

philanthropy — "A desire to improve the material, social and spiritual welfare of humanity especially through charitable services"

Talia got her start as a grassroots leader and philanthropist when she had the idea that kids could trick-or-treat for coins along with candy to help raise money for Hurricane Katrina/Rita relief. Talia used an adult friend's blog, www.halloweenhelpers.blogspot.com, to unite kids across the USA as a philanthropic force. Talia's first endeavor reported over $10 million in relief funding, and ranked the giving power of America's youth with the top five U.S. corporations.

In her ABT interview, Talia talked about the meaning and importance of the RandomKid movement. "I have learned that anyone can do anything if you put your mind to it. That's our tagline: "The Power of Anyone." When you start to tackle something like raising funds for hurricane survivors, you can't imagine how things will turn out. That's OK, because all you need to do is keep your goal in your mind and let the rest happen organically. For example, I learned quickly that "dead end" signs are really "wrong way" signs notifying you that you need to take a different route. Trust me, there is always a route! When I first thought of trick-or-treating for coins along with candy, I wanted kids everywhere to join me. But I saw that other kids wanted to raise money in their own ways . . . like selling lemonade and washing cars. So I decided to link our efforts for a common cause and that yielded a much bigger and better result. But I could never have planned or predicted that outcome. I just had to follow the route that worked, and that led to 10 million dollars and the birth of RandomKid!"

"Now what we do with RandomKid is empower kids by encouraging them to think BIG about everything that matters to them. I want them to know that they can join their project, no matter how big or small, with other kids around the globe who share their goal or passion, and together we can make a BIG difference. We have online chats and conference calls where we plan and brainstorm together, and give the kids the tools they need to get their ideas off the ground. Our role is to empower kids to actually build schools, lay irrigation systems, and place water wells."

"We named the organization RandomKid because that's how I see myself – just a random kid like anyone else, someone who has the power to change the world if I choose to take it on."

RandomKid
The Power of ANYone

BELIEVE IN SOMETHING BIG.

Talia

HUGGABLE HEROES
Talia is a 2007 Build-A-Bear Workshop Huggable Hero

Talia's Insights and Advice:

• Organize yourself or find someone who can organize you.

• Allow your progress to be your energy and your fuel.

• Do it your way – you don't have to be a pro. I wrote my first news release on lined notebook paper with a #2 pencil and faxed it to the TV stations. They took notice because it was different, but the truth is that it was all I knew how to do.

• Believe in yourself – there are no accidents. Your idea came to you because you are the one who can make it happen.

• Remember, as you move toward your goals it gets easier. The path clears as you walk forward.

www.randomkid.org

START SOMETHING BIG.

The ABT interviews you just read have a common theme expressed best by a quote from anthropologist Margaret Mead:

"Never doubt that a small band of thoughtful, committed citizens can change the world — it's the only thing that ever has."

In this case, the small band of committed citizens happened to be kids like you . . . who at age 8 or 9, 10 or 12, 13, 14, or 19 believed in something big. **Their beliefs became their "Mighty Cause". . . Something Big they were willing to stand up for and strive for.** They each committed personal time, energy, and ingenuity to realize results that made the world a better place and in turn made them better and more fulfilled people.

AN IDEA AND A STEP:

It all started with one person's idea and first visible steps. Then others became attracted to the cause, got on board, and contributed their own time, energy, and creativity. **The power of one became the power of many** that created outcomes beyond what anyone imagined or would have thought possible when the idea was born.

YOUR TIME TO BELIEVE:

Take some time to think about what you would do to change the world. Which challenge will you tackle? Which cause will you serve? Which problem will you solve? Which potential will you unleash? Use your mind, heart, and spirit to discover what you most deeply and passionately want for the world. **Believe in Something Big that captures your imagination and commitment.** Take a stand. Join forces with others. Experience the joy, the satisfaction, and the healthy boost in confidence that will be yours by giving the world a chance to change for the better.

CHAPTER 5
SO WHAT'S NEXT?
LET ABT
LEAD THE WAY

YOU ARE READY TO BECOME AN **ABT** TEEN

Cultivating an ABT mindset takes concentrated effort at first because Deficit-Based Thinking is all around us every day. Most news and media reports are DBT. The hallway gossip is DBT. Grading systems in school, coaching practices in sports, the way we evaluate ourselves — our appearance, our popularity, our skills and abilities — almost always lean toward DBT.

When you make the shift from DBT to ABT, you will definitely be swimming upstream at the start. Then, slowly but surely, your passionate effort will pay off. You will instinctively and naturally focus on:

* WHAT'S POSSIBLE   * WHAT'S WORKING
* WHAT'S UNIQUE AND BEST

About you — your relationships and your responsibilities — your life takes on a new aura.

ABT TEENS
WELCOME
TURN HERE ➡

ABT AMAZING:
As an Asset-Based Thinker, you will become:

* MORE RESILIENT
* MORE CREATIVE AND COMPETENT
* MORE CARING AND COMPASSIONATE
* MORE OPTIMISTIC
* MORE CONFIDENT

That's the promise of ABT. That's what's in store for you as a person.

THE WIDER THE LENS, THE BIGGer and BETTer THE vIew:

Until recently, conventional wisdom, scientific research and developmental psychology focused primarily on identifying the factors that put teens at risk. The focus was on preventing and remedying very real dangers and risk factors. While that is important, it only looks at a small part of the picture.

New, groundbreaking research, reported by Dr. Richard Lerner* at Tufts University, shows a bigger picture. Teen years don't have to be a time of sullenness, angst, and rebellion. Their research found that **with the right guidance, teenage years can be healthy, positive, admirable, and productive.** But you already knew that, didn't you? The key is to see what's possible and to encourage what's strong and best about being a teen.

With ABT, you and the adults in your life can work together to realize your potential and recognize the true treasure you are.

* Lerner, R.M., *The Good Teen, Rescuing Adolescence from the Myths of the Storm and Stress Years*: Random House, New York, 2007.

How You **Changed The Way** We See YOU

Creating this book has, beyond a shadow of a doubt, illustrated and illuminated the true treasure and pleasure of interacting and working with teens. So much so that each one of us involved with the book wants to share our new perspectives with you.

In workshops and photo shoots, in group dialogues and interviews, and just hanging out in person and on the Internet, you have shown us the best of who you are. You have opened our eyes to what things mean to you and how much you want to connect with people of all ages – to make your families, schools, communities, and the wider world better. You want and deserve to be listened to and taken seriously.

We applaud you. We celebrate you. We are committed to you. Take a moment to read what all of us want you to know and believe about yourselves. See yourselves through our eyes. Discover through our words of thanks and admiration what you mean to us. Let these words engrave themselves in your mind and heart. *Let ABT lead your way.*

Kathy Cramer

"Since I've listened to your stories, questions and answers, I take your spirit with me everywhere, every day. Thanks for leading and being in my world."

Jeff Hester

"Endeavor to Persevere"

"Discover the unique genius that is in you. That discovery will make you happier and clearer about what you have to contribute to your world."

Judy Dubin

"The optimism and determination I see in you and in my own children encourages me to live my life with that same sense of ABT."

Louise Cadwell

"Young people have the world to offer us. We can listen to their wisdom and insight and move together toward a hopeful, healthy future."

Colleen Moore

"Based on the insightful comments and connections from the youth in our pilot program, ABT will find fertile ground in the teen population."

Penny Allen

Gina Golde

"It's energizing to witness teens connecting and having the courage to share their voices regarding ABT thinking and the possibilities it has to make a difference."

"I have no doubt that our society will reap great rewards as a result of teens' gaining the deep understanding of their unique assets and contributions."

Beth Chesterton

"put your hard work and dedication into your job, but put your genius and soul into your kids"

-Oscar Wilde

John Gellos

"Working with all of you has energized my personal passion for photography even more. Seeing things through your lens has been awesome. Smile!"

Greg Lord

Ben Weinberg

"Your teenage years are crazy and they go so fast that you may lose sight of just how great and important they are."

"I am truly amazed at the positive and enthusiastic response to ABT from these young people. Their ideas and reflections are an inspiration."

Judy Bachman

"Now, more than ever, I wish I was 14 again. I'm convinced you will become the next "Greatest Generation." I can't wait to follow your example."

Hank Wasiak

"You guys have the world by the tail with a downhill pull! And you've made our lives richer for knowing you."

Bettie Schwartz

Amy Miller

"I am constantly amazed by the resilience, creativity and overall awesomeness of young people. It was an honor to be part of this whole project."

"As a planet, we are at a major crossroads. The future leaders, with all of their assets, will choose the right path. I'm sure of it!"

Brian Wasiak

"Your positive intentions and actions gives me hope, purpose and a sense of wonder! You've warmed my heart with your kindness. Thank you!"

Sheila Gurley

Angel Maldonado

"You guys are the beginning of an asset-based thinking generation that will choose to lead by example and create a positive legacy that others may follow on their own journey to success."

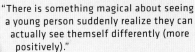

John Davis

"There is something magical about seeing a young person suddenly realize they can actually see themself differently (more positively)."

"ABT takes some of the angst out of the teen years. Doubling the pleasure and halving the worry makes the teen world a great place to be!"

Peggy Guest

"Mind is the Master power that moulds and makes, And Man is Mind, and evermore he takes The tool of Thought, and, shaping what he wills, Brings forth a thousand joys, a thousand ills:— He thinks in secret, and it comes to pass: Environment is but his looking-glass."
                                                    – James Allen

Bryan Sears

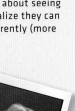

Chuck Contompasis

"Run to a challenge, never from it."

CREDITS

Written by
Kathryn D. Cramer, Ph.D.
Hank Wasiak

Edited by
Kelli Chipponeri

Publicity
Craig Herman

Art direction + design
The Concept Farm

Creative Director
John Gellos

Art Director/Designer
Jeff Hester

Studio Artist
Bryan Sears

Project Manager
Angel Maldonado

Director of Photography
Greg Lord

Workshop Host
The College School

Special Thanks To:

Build-a-Bear Workshop Huggable Heroes

Cassandra Rae – For Carina's Photo

Jan Cramer, the staff and residents at Child Center~Marygrove in St. Louis for delivering incredible pilot workshops

Nancy Margulies - For introducing us to the ABT term "Avocado"

Sherry Dodd - For naming our Mount Rushmore activity

Acknowledgments:

Getty Images

THANKS

To the ABT teens who "knocked our socks off" with their creativity, ingenuity, and unique approach to photography. Their spirit and the images they created permeate every page of this book . . .

Alex Bush	Claire Marcil	Maddy McMullin
Alex Grenius	Claudia Covelli	Matt Gentile
Alex Sith	Daniel Golde	Matthew Moor
Alison Gentile	Daniel Montesdeoca	Maura Corrigan
Amber Jones	Elizabeth Venezia	Merill Morse
Annabelle Cella	Ellen Molinari	Michael Venezia
Brianna Moor	Ezra ("Ezzie")	Moritz Weber
Britney Maldonado	Graham Bhuyan	Nadianna Claunch
Bry Rechan	Inez Mendez	Noah Fuer
Bryanne Leeming	James Robins	Nora Gentile
	Jasmine Plaza	Paige Briscoe
Build-a Bear Workshop® Huggable Heroes	John Hatley	Samantha Romano
Aubyn	John Moor	Sandy Chesterton
Austin	Julia Ross	Sidney Briscoe
Talia	Justin Logan	Thomas Goodkin
Welland	Kevin Haland	Tom Hanson
Zach	Lucas Wasiak	True Morse
Camille Shuken	Lucy Bhuyan	
Carina Gonzalez	Maddy Allnatt	

SEE YOU

VISIT US ON THE

WORLD WIDE WEB

@ ABTTEEN.COM